Discovering Mt.Fuji

富士山

Interpretive Guide Book

CONTENTS

1.	Preface	4
2.	Overview: What is Mt. Fuji?	8
3.	Volcano: A Living Mountain	10
4.	Blessing of Mt. Fuji: Spring Water	28
5.	Beliefs and Folklore Surrounding Mt. Fuji	34
6.	Mt. Fuji in Literature	46
7.	Flora of the Mt. Fuji Habitat	50
8.	Fauna of the Mt. Fuji Habitat	66
9.	Present Condition of Mt. Fuji	84
10.	Mountain Climbing Information	86
11.	Closing Remarks	92

1.Preface

If you were to take a survey of people around the world, asking what image comes to mind when they think of Japan, most of them would probably reply "Mt. Fuji." Many visitors from abroad come to Japan for various reasons such as travel and business, but often without any intent to actually climb this most famous mountain. However, some do decide that since they are already in Japan, it would be a pity not to see Mt. Fuji at least once before they leave.

To the Japanese people, Mt. Fuji is a solitary mountain peak, a beautiful sloping skyscraper, that has become the most beloved mountain of all. This sacred mountain is not only the provider of many blessings for us, but its very presence commands a sense of awe and respect.

I have been an ecotourism interpreter (that is, a guide), both domestically and overseas, for over 15 years. And my coauthor, Mr. ToshioTagami, has also been an interpreter through his art. In this case, interpreting does not mean merely showing people the way, and explaining natural phenomena; it refers to being guides who aim at providing a deeper sense of feeling and understanding for their subject. We do this by giving a thorough explanation of the hidden significance behind the natural culture and events of a particular land, as well as of their relationship to their surroundings.

It is a pity that, of the 300,000 visitors who come to Mt. Fuji every year during climbing season, many have passed over it without even recognizing that they had been in the presence of a rich and profound natural environment.

It is our wish through this book, to provide a greater understanding of how Japanese people think about Mt. Fuji, and of how living beings-both human and animal-continue to live in the presence of the mighty nature around Mt. Fuji.

Author : Masanori Shintani

1.Preface

Spring 春

夏 Summer

Autumn 秋

Winter 冬

What is an interpretation?

"Interpretation is a mission-based communication process that forges emotional and intellectual connections between the interests of the audience and the meanings inherent in the resource." (National Association for Interpretation)

At present, interpretation has been widely used as an effective technique for ecotourism and environmental education by interpreters at national parks, World Heritage sites, museums, and scenic locations all over the world.

2. Overview: What is Mt. Fuji?

Altitude (Kengamine Peak Summit)
At 3,776 meters (12,388 feet) above sea level, it is Japan's highest mountain.

Circumference
- At Mountain's Base: 153 km (95 miles)
- At 2,500 meters (8,202 feet)
  above sea level: 17 km (10.6 miles)
- At Summit Crater: 3 km (1.9 miles) (p.20)

Position (Kengamine Peak Summit)
- Longitude: 138° 45′ 1″ E
- Latitude: 35° 21′ 5″ N

Mt. Fuji is located in the middle of the Japanese Archipelago.

Status of Volcanic Activity
Mt. Fuji is an active volcano, though it is currently classified as being at low risk for eruption. It is a tall, conical mountain composed of basalt lava, cinders, and ash in alternating layers, the products of different types of eruptions. This type of volcano is called a stratovolcano.

Ownership
- The northern side: Yamanashi prefecture
- The southern side: Shizuoka prefecture
- 8th station until the top: the shrine,
  Fujisan Hongu Sengen Taisha (p.35)

National Park

Mt. Fuji is designated as "Fuji Hakone Izu National Park" and encompasses specially protected areas such as that above the 5th station, and "Aokigahara Sea of Trees" (p.62), where you are prohibited from taking any rocks or plants home with you.

"Take Only Pictures, Leave Only Footprints".

Method for Designating Height

Mt. Fuji is divided up into ten 合目 (or "go-me," which means "stations"). The base of Mt. Fuji is 1 Gome, and so on until the top, which is 10 Gome. The gomes are not evenly spaced out by distance nor by elevation. Some say the distance is the length or amount of time it would take to burn out one 合 (go = 0.18 liters) worth of oil in a Japanese traditional lantern. Others say it is the distance it would take to slowly empty out a 1 go wooden cup full of uncooked rice.

5 Gome can be reached by car.

Where Did Mt. Fuji's Name Come From?

Opinions differ on how Mt. Fuji's name originated. One theory comes from the Japanese wording "不二" (pronounced fu-ji and meaning "Only One"), and another comes from the wording "不死" (also pronounced fu-ji and meaning "Never Die"). (p.47)

3. Volcano: A Living Mountain

Plate Tectonics

The surface of our earth is made up of tectonic plates. These plates are somewhat like the thin layer of "skin" which forms if you leave heated milk sitting out for a while. The "milk" can be likened to the magma which lies within the belly of the earth. The way these plates interact with each other resembles the outer surface of a soccer ball, with each plate able to rise and sink in various directions repeatedly. The ground on which Mt. Fuji sits comes in contact with four different tectonic plates: the Eurasian plate, the Filipino plate, the North American plate, and the Pacific plate. Due to its volatile position here, this is considered one of the world's most geologically unique locations.

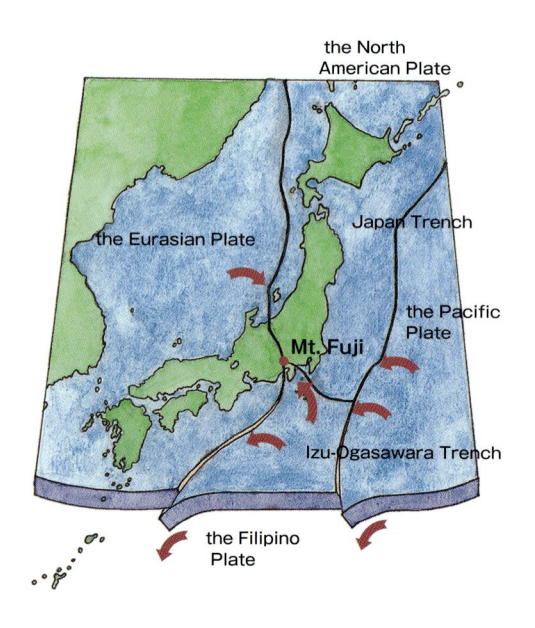

The Birth of Mt. Fuji

Scientists today believe that the occurrence of earthquakes in Japan is connected to the movement of tectonic plates. For example, when the plates slowly subduct under the Japanese archipelago from the East, then the friction of the plates creates tension which, when it becomes too great, causes the plates to jolt suddenly and cause an earthquake.

In fact, the emergence of Mt. Fuji is deeply related to the subduction of tectonic plates. As the plates sank deeply, the rise in pressure and temperature caused part of the upper mantle to melt, which created magma. This magma then slowly rose up through the earth, where it is thought to have emerged from the earth's surface between 100 and 200 thousand years ago.

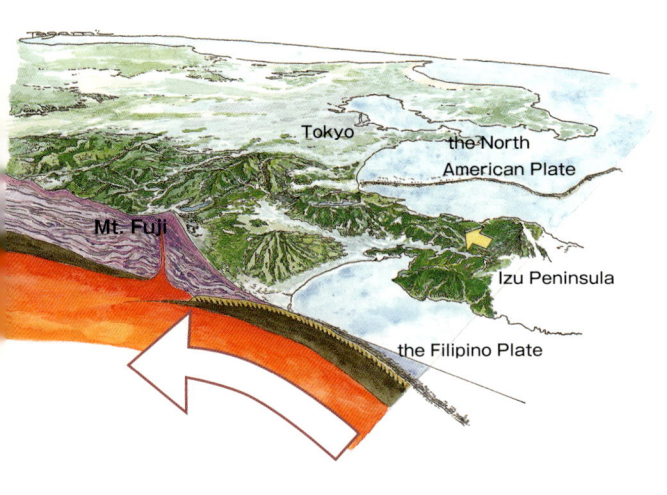

3. Volcano: A Living Mountain

The Growth of Mt. Fuji

Mt. Fuji is a stratovolcano consisting of three volcanoes*, listed here in decreasing order of age.

Komitake Volcano: Some 100 to 200 thousand years ago, it emerged on the northern side of where Mt. Fuji lies today. It was made of relatively high viscosity "andesite" lava.

Ko-Fuji (Old Fuji) Volcano: Due to a process of repeatedly erupting and collapsing, this volcano developed at the midway of Komitake, on the site of the present Mt. Fuji, around 100 thousand years ago.

Shin-Fuji (Young Fuji) Volcano: About 10 thousand years ago, eruptions began again, resulting in the formation of the current shape of Mt. Fuji. The lava was a runny "basalt" composite.

*Recently, scientists also found another old volcano, referred to as "Pre-Komitake" under Komitake, so there are now presumed to be four volcanoes composing Mt. Fuji.

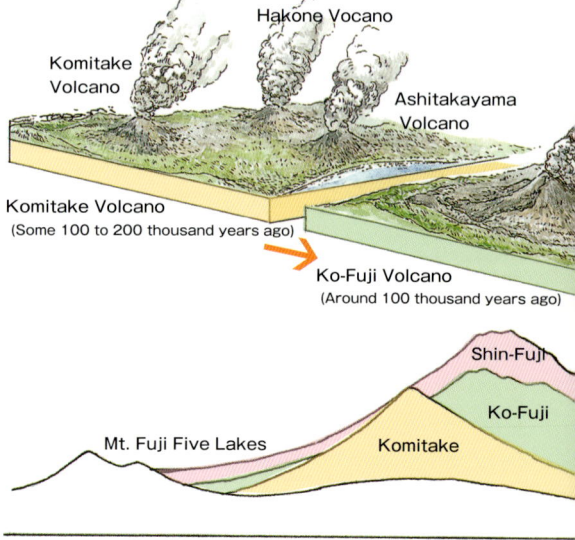

Hakone Vocano
Komitake Volcano
Ashitakayama Volcano

Komitake Volcano
(Some 100 to 200 thousand years ago)

Ko-Fuji Volcano
(Around 100 thousand years ago)

Shin-Fuji
Ko-Fuji
Mt. Fuji Five Lakes
Komitake

N
Yamanashi Side

Catching a Glimpse of Ko-Fuji Volcano

It is possible to see Ko-Fuji (Old Fuji) Volcano at the right shoulder of Houei Crater (p.18). About 300 years ago, it erupted explosively and pushed to the surface of Shin-Fuji the portion of Ko-Fuji which can now be seen. This portion is called "Aka-Iwa" meaning "Red-Rock." It is thought that the black basalt lava contained iron, and became red over time due to the oxidation of the metal content and the exposure to extreme heat from the eruption.

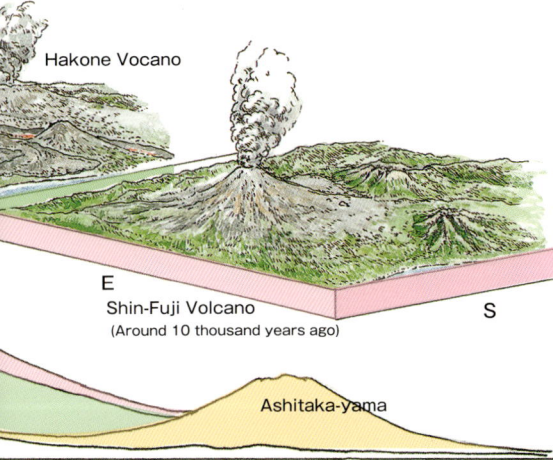

Hakone Vocano

E
Shin-Fuji Volcano
(Around 10 thousand years ago)
S

Ashitaka-yama

S
Shizuoka Side

3. Volcano: A Living Mountain

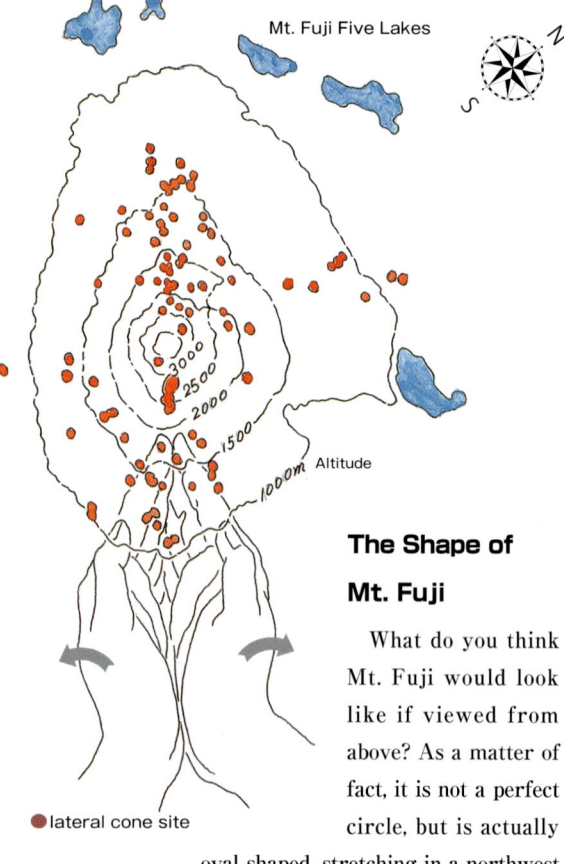

Mt. Fuji Five Lakes

1000m Altitude

● lateral cone site

The Shape of Mt. Fuji

What do you think Mt. Fuji would look like if viewed from above? As a matter of fact, it is not a perfect circle, but is actually oval shaped, stretching in a northwest to southeast direction. This is due to the force enacted by the movement of the plate from the northeast, when the path of the magma and the lava flowed in an almost straight direction. Then, the magma flowed repeatedly through the volcanic vent and built up Mt Fuji.

To get a picture of what this might have looked like, try bringing your palms together and then pressing your fingertips against the wall.

Interestingly, if you look carefully at Mt. Fuji from the east or west side, you can see some cones along the line of the mountain ridge. (See the picture below).

Photo: Yamanashi Institute of Environmental Sciences

Cones along the line of Mt. Fuji ridge

These are called "soku-kazan" meaning "lateral cones." These cinder (scoria) cones are small volcanic mountains created by volcanic eruptions at the foot or middle of a mountain, or at any other point besides the summit crater. Scientists have found more than 100 cones on Mt. Fuji at present. This helps us understand how active Mt. Fuji was.

3. Volcano: A Living Mountain

Various Side Views of Mt. Fuji

People living around Mt. Fuji always say that the best view of Mt. Fuji is from their side. Of course, they have been admiring it since their childhood. This is a really wonderful thing. Because Mt. Fuji stretches in an oblong direction, depending on the angle from which we view it, the shape and the width may vary dramatically. The view may also change dramatically depending on the season and time of day in which you see it. This offers yet another way to cherish and appreciate Mt. Fuji's unique beauty. Which side of Mt. Fuji do you like best?

東 *East*

西 *West*

Interpretive GuideBook

北
North

南
South

Is Mt. Fuji Cracking?

On Mt. Fuji's western slope, there is a big crevasse called the "Osawa fault." It reaches a surprising depth of 150 meters (492 feet), and is primarily the result of erosion by the rain and west wind. The average total amount of sediment eroded is estimated to be about thirty 10-ton truckloads a day.

3.Volcano: A Living Mountain

Houei Crater

Houei Crater is also a "lateral cone" (p.15) on Mt. Fuji, and presents a dynamic and aesthetically appealing image of a volcanic eruption. Around 300 years ago, in 1707, there was one of the largest volcanic eruptions on this location. In fact, the eruption continued for sixteen days. The volcanic ashes reached all the way to Tokyo (Edo), about 150 kilometers (93 miles) from Mt. Fuji, and are said to have caused a lot of damage to the area. Houei Crater is made up of three different craters, the largest of which is over 1.3 kilometer (0.8mile) in circumference. The origin of the name of Houei Crater is derived from the original Japanese naming system based on the year and era. Because the eruption happened during the Houei Era, it thus received its current name. To see Houei Crater for yourself, there is a great 2 hour round trip trekking course from the Fujinomiya entrance. Make sure you try it out!!

Houei 1st Crater

The Legend of Ina Hanzaemon
(Houei Volcanic Eruption)

During the Houei volcanic eruption, farmers in the eastern foothills of Mt. Fuji, having had their fields buried, were simply awaiting death. At that time, the acting administrative guardian of the area was Ina Hanzaemon. Having seen the desperate condition the villagers were in, he attempted to help them by distributing stored rice according to his own judgment. When his actions became known to the officials, he was sentenced to life imprisonment in exile on an island. Not accepting his sentence, he is said to have then committed suicide by Harakiri. His great deed has been passed down from generation to generation for over 300 years.

3. Volcano: A Living Mountain

Summit Crater

At the top of Mt. Fuji, there is a huge created by several hundred past volcanic eruptions, which were then followed by one last huge eruption which occurred around 2,200 years ago before it began to quiet down.

- Diameter: about 600 meters (1970 feet)
- Depth: about 200 meters (656feet),
- Circumference: about 3 kilometers (1.86 miles)

Crater on top of Mt. Fuji, "Ohachi"

In Japan, because the shape of the crater looks very much like the shape of a bowl, it is called a "hachi" which means "bowl." The crater has eight peaks, with each peak being the sanctuary of a god, so that once we have walked around the entire circumference, or "completely rounded the bowl," it is believed that

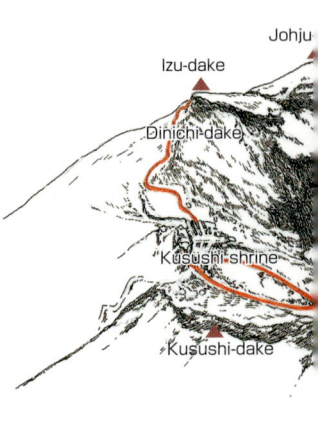

Johju
Izu-dake
Dinichi-dake
Kusushi-shrine
Kusushi-dake

Interpretive GuideBook

we will be blessed.

This round trip takes two hours. If you have enough time and energy, please try it for your blessing.

On the top of Mt. Fuji, there are two shrines standing at the end of the trails from the Fujinomiya and the Gotenba entrances (called the Okumiya shrine) and from the Subashiri and the Yoshida/the Kawaguchiko entrances (called the Kusushi Shrine). Many worshippers pay their respects at both shrines. Both the Okumiya and the Kusushi shrines have two nearby snowmelt springs, where water passes through volcanic lava. These are called "Ginmei-sui" (which means "Silver Water") and "Kinmei-sui" (which means "Gold Water"), and people have enshrined them as blessed sites.

In addition, there are permanently-frozen soils on the mountaintop, and some lichens and mosses have adapted to live in this special area. Unfortunately, it is believed that they have also been diminishing with each passing year due to the effects of global warming.

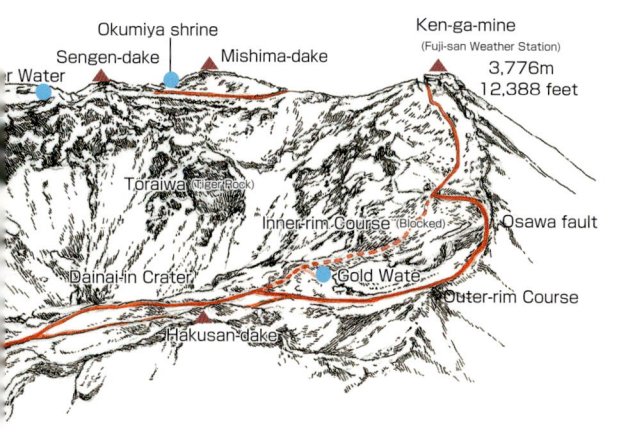

3.Volcano: A Living Mountain

Lava

Lava is magma that bursts through the surface of the earth, and then flows out from within. This is sort of like when a person gets injured and blood, like magma, bursts from the blood vessels and flows out through the broken skin, like the earth's crust, to form a scab. This scab is like the volcano. In fact, because magma is always flowing around inside the earth, we could almost say that the earth is like a living being.

Hawaii Volcanoes National Park

The lava of Mt. Fuji is basaltic, which contains around 50% silicon dioxide. The temperature of the lava is around 1,100°C (1,950°F), and when it reaches the surface-because of the dramatic temperature difference with the air-unless the flow is fast enough, the lava will cool rapidly and harden to black. Also, the lava has rock small bubbles in it. When gases inside the magma reach the surface of the earth, the gas pressure rapidly drops and bubbles form as it hardens-ust like when you shake a carbonated drink and then open it, spewing out bubbles.

High heat basaltic lava emerges to the surface of the earth, where it creates new land. The form of the lava changes according to different conditions.

Let me introduce some of the lava forms that can be seen around Mt. Fuji.

Pahoehoe

Its name comes from the Hawaiian word meaning "smooth" and it has a smooth, fluid appearance.

Hawaii Volcanoes National Park

Aa

Aa means "rocky" in Hawaiian, and it is characteristically rough and bumpy, being made up primarily of broken lava blocks.

Block

This is formed when a thick flow of lava cools and hardens.

3. Volcano: A Living Mountain

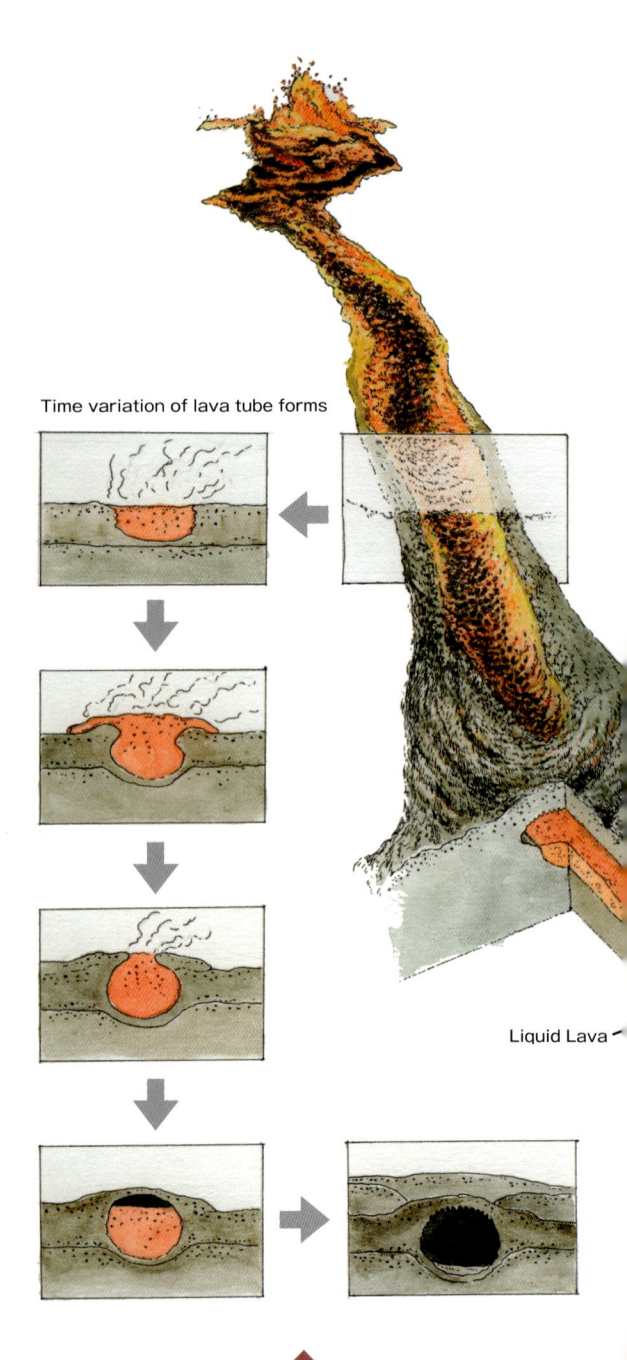

Time variation of lava tube forms

Liquid Lava

Interpretive GuideBook

Volcanic Caves

Did you know that Mt. Fuji actually contains one of the world's highest concentrations of lava caves?

Several caves may be observed at the foot of Mt. Fuji, but in the northern area of the "Aokigahara Sea of Trees" (p. 62) more than one hundred lava caves have been discovered. The caves in the area where greenery is covering the woodland were created around 1,100 years ago (in the year 864) when an eruption occurred. Though it appears to be primarily forest, many groups of lava caves exist below ground.

By the way, volcanic caves are different from "limestone caves," which are slowly produced as precipitation seeps through the ground and creates calcium carbonate formations.

How Lava Caves are Created

A lava cave, or lava tube, is formed from flowing pahoehoe lava. Though the lava's outer surface hardens on contact with the air, the inside keeps flowing. Once it has stopped, a long horizontal tube remains, similar to a cast-off snake skin.

Solid Lava

Stalactites

Pahoehoe
The tip of liquid lava flow chills in order and develop rope-like lava.

3. Volcano: A Living Mountain

Mystery of Caves

The underground world, with nearly no light coming through, is totally different from the world we live in above the surface. Inside the cave, structures remain largely unchanged from the time they were first formed by the hardening lava flow, almost as though time had stood still. When scalding hot lava flowed along its course, the cave ceiling would have started to melt,

Lava Stalactites

forming "lava stalactites" like nipples in different places. And when the rains fell, water flowed along the trees, mosses, lichens, soils and lava cracks, and down along the lava stalactites dripping into the cave. One can imagine it would have been almost like the performance of a water drop orchestra. This world down below, within the lava caves, is truly amazing.

Among these low temperature caves, there are also caves with icicles (known as "ice caves").

Tree Molds

During a volcanic eruption, lava would flow steadily through the trees of the forest. When this occurred, the trees were engulfed by lava and set aflame. Later, the hot lava would cool, leaving vertical tree molds in place, which preserved the original shape of the trees. If the trees could not withstand the force of the flow, they would have been knocked down, which would result in a horizontal tree mold, similar in appearance to a lava cave.

Note: As caves may be quite dangerous, it is strongly recommended that an ecotour guide accompany you when exploring any caves.

4.Blessing of Mt. Fuji: Spring Water

Mt. Fuji, a Huge Water Jar

Mt. Fuji, to us, is the provider of many blessings. One of the most precious of these is our water. Mt. Fuji as a whole is said to receive 2.2 billion tons of precipitation each year, yet we see no rivers flowing around the mountain. So where does the water go? Scientists believe that the rain seeps slowly through the Shin-Fuji Volcano, all the way to the layers of Old-Fuji. However, a mud "filter" allows only slow, relatively poor penetration (p.12)

The water continues to push through the layers of sediment, and eventually bursts out into the Mt. Fuji

Shiraito Falls (Fujinomiya city)

surroundings as spring water. Mt. Fuji is, in someways, a "mountain of water." Furthermore, the mosses and soils of the forest provide us with water that is rich in minerals. They also help prevent erosion thanks to their role as a natural dam of sorts, which slows water penetration.

One of the most famous waterfalls in Japan, beautiful Shiraito Falls is so named because its trails of water resemble "white threads." Thousands of small streams trickle through the layers of Mt. Fuji, and the number of waterfalls increases in the springtime due to the melting snow.

4. Blessing of Mt. Fuji: Spring Water

Shiraito Falls

Oshino-hakkai

Shiraito Falls

Wakutama Pond

Wakutama Pond

Around Mt. Fuji is a Treasure House of Spring Water

As you can see in this figure, there are many springs among the surroundings of Mt. Fuji, which benefit local people for their personal use in daily life, agriculture, industry, and more.

However, these activities are beginning to cause concern due to the way they are depleting the spring water system fed by the groundwater being pumped up through holes in the lava layers. We really need to devote more study to the groundwater system, and form an appropriate, sustainable plan. Without a doubt, this water is something that must be kept clean; it is a precious treasure to be preserved and passed on to the next generation.

Oshino-hakkai

Kakitagawa River

Kakitagawa River

"Japanese Saké" of Mt. Fuji Tastes So Good.

No great saké is made without great water. Most saké cellars maintain their same tried-and-true manufacturing methods for making delicious saké from their rice crop. This is a perfect combination of wisdom and thought from those who make saké, coupled with the essence of blessing from Mt. Fuji.

Photo: Fuji-nishiki Brewery

4. Blessing of Mt. Fuji: Spring Water

Mt. Fuji Five Lakes (Fuji-goko)

At the northern side of Mt. Fuji in Yamanashi prefecture are the Five Lakes of Mt. Fuji (Lake Yamanaka, Lake Kawaguchi, Lake Sai, Lake Shoji, and Lake Motosu). Many people come to visit this region, simply to enjoy the striking image of beautiful Mt. Fuji reflected in the lake. These lakes are classified as "Dammed Lakes," which were formed as water was stopped up by the lava from a volcanic eruption. In the year 864 when Mt. Nagao erupted, the lava flow (the "Aokigahara lava flow") separated a lake called "Senoumi" into Lake Sai and Lake Shoji, and formed the current shape that we can still see today.

Currently, because the water levels of Lake Sai, Lake Shoji, and Lake Motosu are of the same height, they are thought to connect underground.

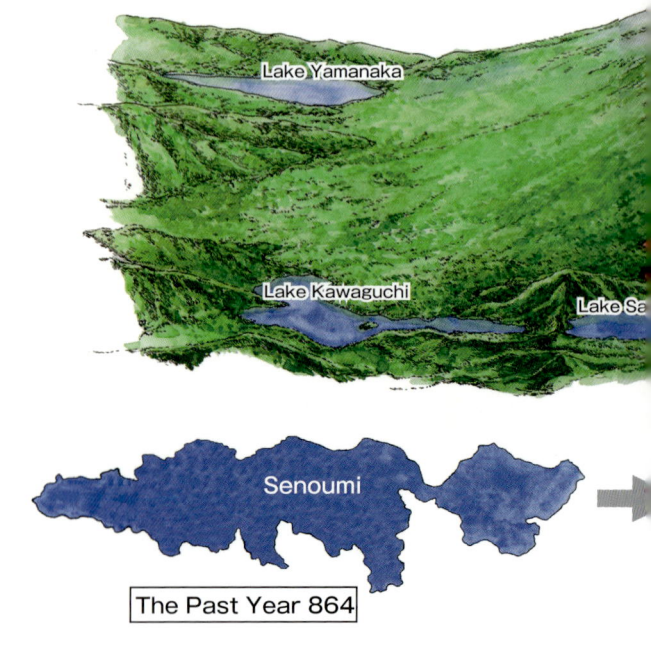

The Past Year 864

Interpretive GuideBook

Lake Motosu: found on the 1,000 yen note

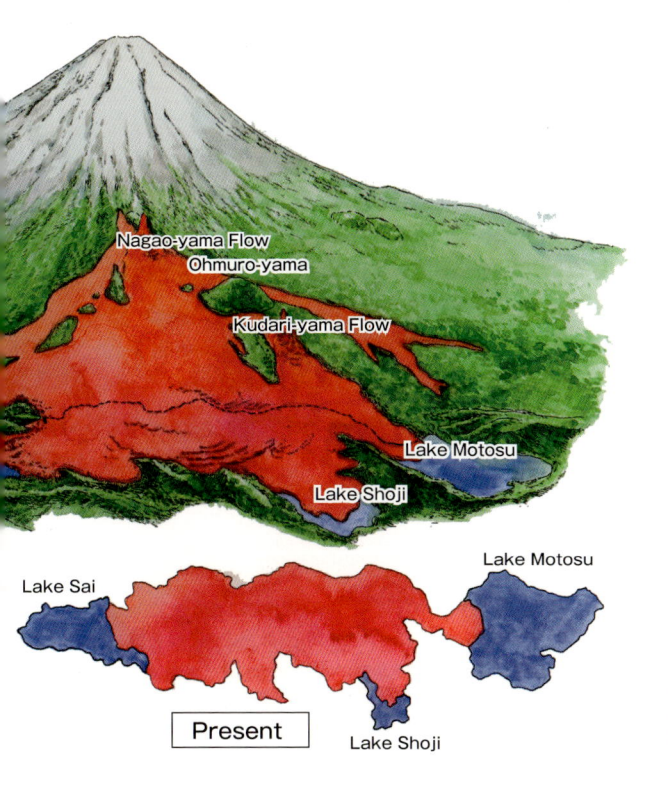

Nagao-yama Flow
Ohmuro-yama
Kudari-yama Flow
Lake Motosu
Lake Shoji

Lake Sai
Lake Motosu
Present
Lake Shoji

5. Beliefs and Folklore Surrounding Mt. Fuji

Shintoism

Sometimes nature strikes us with disaster. Japan in particular is a country that is never far removed from natural disasters like typhoons, earthquakes, and volcanic activity. Towards these overwhelming forces of nature the Japanese people are fearful, respectful, and worshipful of them as gods. The belief in the existence of numerous gods dwelling in everything such as mountains, rivers, and even water have spread throughout the land and developed into the native Japanese belief of "Shintoism." Shinto shrines stand in many areas all throughout Japan. Even today, seasonal Shinto festivals are held to celebrate a good harvest, and to thank the gods responsible.

Mountain God (Nishiusuzuka, Mt.Fuji)

Fujisan Hongu Sengen Taisha
(Shrine)

This place of worship for the Shinto god Sengen Taisha, which is also the foremost of more than a thousand Sengen shrines throughout Japan, is located in Fujinomiya, Shizuoka prefecture. The story of its origin tells that, in order to

The front shrine

calm the "fire" (volcanic lava) within Mt. Fuji that erupted from time to time, Emperor Suinin, in 27 B.C., worshipped Mt. Fuji as the body of the god itself. The main deity of the Sengen shrine is Konohana-sakuyahime. Esteemed as a model for all Japanese women, she personifies the virtues of beauty and gentleness (p.39).

5. Beliefs and Folklore Surrounding Mt. Fuji

The current buildings were constructed in 1604 by Shogun Tokugawa Ieyasu. Despite partial dismantling and renovation over the centuries, the inner shrine, the front shrine, and the tower gate all appear exactly the way they did when built, and the inner shrine has been designated an important cultural property.

The inner shrine

Wakutama-Ike (Pond)

Within the shrine lies a pond where spring water gushes out. People believe that the shrine was located at this area to worship Konohana-sakuyahime as a virtuous god of water that calms fire. In former times, when there were a great number of devoted Fuji confraternities known as "Fujikou" (p.42), they would purify themselves with this holy water before entering the mountain. This purification rite still occurs annually, on the day of the official opening of the Mt. Fuji climbing season.

Kitaguchi Hongu Fuji Sengen Jinja
(North Entrance Fuji Head Sengen Shrine)

This Sengen shrine sits tucked away in a cedar forest in Fujiyoshida, Yamanashi prefecture. The shrine was originally established in 110 A.D. and its inner shrine was built in 1615 in hopes of suppressing the volcanic activities. An 18 meter (60 foot) tall wooden gate or "torii" marks the official entrance, and two gigantic Japanese cedar trees, called "sugi" (p.65) - both over 1,000 years old - flank it like guards on either side. Traditionally, pilgrims to Mt. Fuji's summit would begin their journey here. Considered by locals to be one of the most eccentric festivals in Japan, the Himatsuri Fire Festival, announces the official end of the Mt. Fuji climbing season. Held here on August 26th and 27th of every year, the main attraction of the festival is over eighty 3 meter tall flaming torches, which line Showa Douri St. from Kanadorii torii gate to Sengen Jinja.

Himatsuri Fire Festival
Photo:Fujiyoshida Kankou-shinkou Service

5. Beliefs and Folklore Surrounding Mt. Fuji

Okumiya (Shrine on top of Mt. Fuji)

Since ancient times, the area above the eighth station of Mt. Fuji (nearly four square kilometers, 1.5 square miles) has been the precinct of Okumiya shrine, which is managed by the Fujisan Hongu Sengen Shrine. The Okumiya shrine awaits pilgrims on top of the mountain, at the end of the trail from the Fujinomiya and the Gotenba entrances. There is no inner shrine, but only outer and middle shrines, since Mt. Fuji itself is the god's body.

Okumiya
Photo:Fujinomiya City

Kusushi Shrine

This branch of the Okumiya shrine stands at the end of the trails ascending from the Subashiri and the Yoshida/the Kawaguchiko entrances.

Many worshippers climb up to the top of Mt. Fuji and pay their respects at both shrines, carrying various wishes with them.

Princess
Konohana-sakuyahime

According to Japanese mythological literature, the princess was a daughter of Oyamazumi, the mountain god. Once upon a time a god, Ninigi-no-mikoto, saw the princess and wanted to marry her. After they spent the night together, he then departed for a journey. One year later, after coming back from his journey, Mikoto saw the pregnant princess and was suspicious about whether the princess was having his baby. He then asked the princess "after spending one night with me, whose baby is it that you are having?" The princess, to prove her innocence, replied, "If they are your offspring, I shall have no problem giving birth in the fire." She then set fire to her birthing room. After that, she successfully gave birth to three children in the furiously burning fire, and therefore proved her innocence. For that, she is known as a goddess who protects against various kinds of fire like that from volcanic eruptions, and she is also considered the goddess of safe maternity.

5. Beliefs and Folklore Surrounding Mt. Fuji

Fuji Mandara (Devotional Paintings of Mt. Fuji)
Fujisan Hongu Sengen Taisha Collection

Time went on, and during the Heian Era (794~1185) Mt. Fuji, instead of being only adored from a distance, became the site for practicing a form of mountain asceticism known as "Shugendou." This devotional painting of Mt. Fuji in a large scroll picture was believed to have been drawn by Kano Motonobu at the end of the Muromachi Era (1336~1573). The mountain peak, which the pilgrims are aiming for, is the heavenly paradise (or "jodo"), which is being protected by three statues of Buddhist images.

The pilgrims are to participate in a water purification ceremony at the Sengen shrine.

At that time, females were forbidden to participate, so for that reason no women can be seen above the mountain's midway point.

Also, because of their very early morning departure, they would have brought a torch to climb the mountain.

5. Beliefs and Folklore Surrounding Mt. Fuji

Fujikou (Devotional Fuji Confraternities)

At the beginning of the Edo period (1603~1867), Fujikou, the devotional Fuji confraternities, spread to Edo and its surrounding provinces. Wishing for happiness, health, and the prosperity of their families, the act of climbing Mt. Fuji became a popular show of faith.

The Legend of Kakugyo

Hasegawa Kakugyo (1541~1646), purported to be the original founder of Fujikou, is said to have completed 1,000 days of ascetic practices inside the Hitoana cave at the base of Mt. Fuji, standing on a 14 cm square timber(5.5 inches) inside a watery cave. After such austerities, he is said to have reached enlightenment and therefore laid the foundation of Fujikou. This cave still exists in Fujinomiya city and has been carefully protected as a holy place.

Rokkon Shojou (Purification of the Six Senses)

Since olden days, pilgrims have chanted the Rokkon Shojou, under the influence of Buddhism, while climbing the mountain. The Rokkon are the eyes, ears, nose, tongue, body, and mind through which humans indulge their greed. Climbing the mountain offers a means of purification for devotees, and even today some people chant the Rokkon Shojou while climbing.

Fujizuka (Fuji City)

Fujizuka (Mt. Fuji Mound)

Climbing Mt. Fuji became a status symbol for people in the Edo period. However, women and unwell people were forbidden to climb. Therefore, "Mt. Fuji Mounds", or piles of sand and rocks, were built and regarded as sacred throughout Japan, and can still be seen today in various locations.

5. Beliefs and Folklore Surrounding Mt. Fuji

Haibutsu Kishaku

(Abolition of Buddhism)

You might imagine that Shinto and Buddhism existed in harmony side by side on Mt. Fuji. However, in 1868 the Meiji government announced an official policy separating Shinto and Buddhism, which led to the destruction of Buddhist temples, images, and texts around the nation. The Sengen shrines around Mt. Fuji also came

Defaced Buddhist images(top of Mt.Fuji)

under the influence of the abolition, and many Buddhist images in Mt.Fuji were destroyed and dumped into the crater.

Even though Buddhist culture has since been revived, defaced stone images enshrined obscurely on top of Mt. Fuji continue to tell us this story as a warning not to repeat this sad history.

The First Woman Climber

In the Edo period, women were not permitted access to the mountain. In the year 1832, a woman named Ms. Tatsu Takayama, dressed like a man, became the first woman to successfully climb to the summit of Mt. Fuji. The prohibition was removed in 1872.

The First Foreign Climber

In 1860, the first British ambassador to Japan, Sir Rutherford Alcock, became the first foreigner to successfully reach Mt. Fuji's summit. For the Japanese people, Mt. Fuji was a heart sanctuary, which meant that many at that time opposed the idea of a foreigner climbing the mountain. The government was also very much against the idea, for safety's sake. But in spite of numerous obstacles, Sir Alcock's climb to the top ended successfully, with great enthusiasm. Because of many people's passion over the course of history, now anybody-regardless of age, gender, nationality, or religion-can climb Mt. Fuji. Perhaps your view of Mt. Fuji has changed too, having learned some of its history.

Sir Alcock
(Fujinomiya-guchi, Shin 5 Gome)

6. Mt. Fuji in Literature

For the Japanese, Mt. Fuji is a special natural and cultural site; therefore, a great amount of literature has been written about it. Some poets have likened different aspects of the volcano to human lives and emotions.

Tago no ura yu Uchi idete mireba

Mashironi so Fuji no takane ni

Yuki wa furi keru

(When I took the path through Tago Bay and reached the area with a view, the lofty peak of Mt. Fuji was covered by pure white snow.)

Yamabe no Akahito

Manyoshu poetry anthology
(7~8 century)

Kaze ni nabiku Fuji no kemuri no

Sora ni kiete Yukue mo shiranu

Waga omoi kana

(My feeling is going to somewhere, as if the windblown smoke of Mt. Fuji disappears into the sky.)

Saigyo

Shin Kokin Wakashu poetry anthology
(13 century)

Kaguyahime (Princess Kaguya)

Once upon a time, there lived a happy old couple at the foot of Mt. Fuji. One day, when the couple went out to collect bamboo, the man found a shining bamboo, and when it was cracked open, a lovely little girl came out from inside. The old couple, who had no children, then named the child "Kaguyahime," and raised the child very carefully as though she was a gift from God. As time went by, she grew to become a beautiful girl, attracting five suitors from noble and imperial families to request her hand in marriage, but she (with difficulty) continued rejecting them, until finally she returned to Mt. Fuji. The emperor, who had received a medicine for "eternal life" from Kaguyahime, having said that it was hopeless to try to live without her, is said to have burnt the medicine at the mountain summit.

Therefore, some say this mountain was named "Fu-ji" meaning "Never Die."

6.Mt. Fuji in Literature

Ukiyoe「Katsushika Hokusai」

There are probably a lot of people who have seen this picture at least once. This was one of the world-famous ukiyoe (wood block) prints created by the artist Hokusai

Hokusai (1760〜1849)

The world-class impressionist painter Vincent Van Gogh and the French composer Claude Debussy are both said to have gained inspiration from Hokusai's paintings.

at the age of 70. His famous Fugaku 36 kei ("thirty-six views of Mt. Fuji") depicts Mt. Fuji as a powerful theme in the Edo period.

Sanka Hakuu (Red Storm beneath the Summit)

The red lightning flashed and the thunder rumbled intensely. However, snow-capped Mt. Fuji remained calm, maintaining its still appearance. This painting is also called "Black Fuji." You can imagine that the people living on the skirt of Mt. Fuji must have been thrown into a panic by the strong rain.

7. Flora of the Mt. Fuji Habitat

Vertical Distribution Chart of Flora

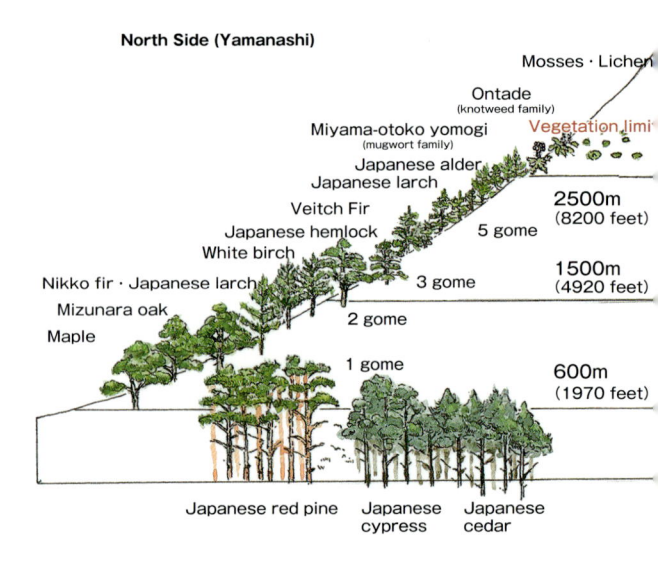

North Side (Yamanashi)

Mosses · Lichen
Ontade (knotweed family)
Miyama-otoko yomogi (mugwort family)
Vegetation limit
Japanese alder
Japanese larch
Veitch Fir
Japanese hemlock
White birch
5 gome
2500m (8200 feet)
Nikko fir · Japanese larch
3 gome
1500m (4920 feet)
Mizunara oak
Maple
2 gome
1 gome
600m (1970 feet)

Japanese red pine | Japanese cypress | Japanese cedar

Flora

When traveling to the fifth station (about 2,300〜2,400 meters, or 7,546〜7,874 feet) by vehicle, please take notice of the changes in the forest around you along the way. You will see that the trees change along with the altitude. The change in distribution of plants in this manner, according to the change in altitude, is referred to as "vertical distribution." This can be seen dramatically at Mt. Fuji, which acts almost like a natural museum!

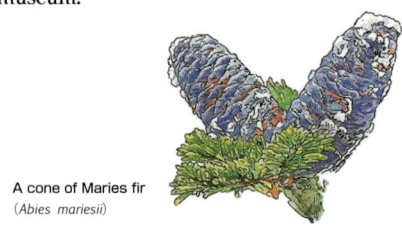

A cone of Maries fir
(*Abies mariesii*)

Interpretive GuideBook

3776m
(12388 feet)

South Side (Shizuoka)

Mosses · Lichens

Ontade (knotweed family)

Vegetation limit

Japanese larch

Japanese alder

Japanese larch

Gold birch

Shin 5 gome

Japanese hemlock

Subalpine zone

Veitch Fir

Nikko fir

Japanese larch

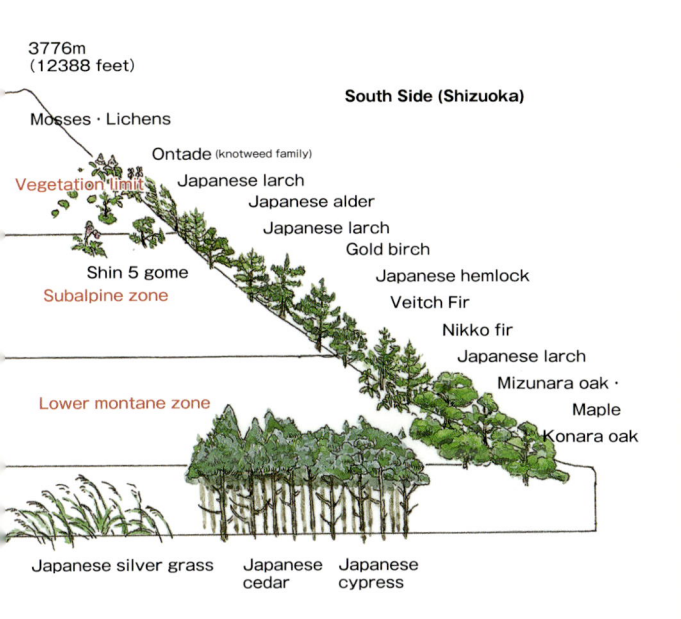

Lower montane zone

Mizunara oak ·

Maple

Konara oak

Japanese silver grass   Japanese cedar   Japanese cypress

The selection of vegetation on the north side varies slightly from that on the south side. On the south side, the plants love sunlight, whereas the north side is inhabited by plants preferring shade from the sun. Plants live by adapting to the slightest change in their environment, such as temperature, light, and humidity. If we look above the fifth station, we can no longer see large trees. This is the altitude where plants can no longer live as a forest, and it is called the "vegetation limit." Why not try an extended walk around the fifth station?

A cone of Japanese larch
(*Larix Kaempferi*)

7.Flora of the Mt. Fuji Habitat

Patches turned yellow in Autumn

Plants Above the Vegetation Limit (Alpine Zone)

There are some harsh environmental factors at this area: the temperature variance both within a day and in between seasons, the short time frame (from spring to fall) for plants to be able to live, the strong daily wind, the gap between rainy and sunny days, and so on. Moreover, the landscape is made of scoria (volcanic pumice stone) that slips and slides, having a devastating impact on plants. The plants, even in such a severe environment, have managed to survive by adapting to their surroundings.

Alpine & Subalpine Zone

10mm
(0.4inches)

Scoria

Patches

You might be curious about the many aggregates of grasses above the fifth station. These are called "patches." Fortuitously, the wind carries away some of the grass seeds, which allows new stems to sprout elsewhere, thus extending the lifespan of the patches.

7.Flora of the Mt. Fuji Habitat

Ontade (*Aconogonum weyrichii var. alpinum*)
Polygonaceae, Aconogonum
Height: 20〜80cm (7.8〜31.5 inches)

The ontade, which lives in the alpine zone, has a lifespan of only two and a half months, being among the slowest plants to sprout up and the fastest to drop its leaves. During its life, it produces offspring and stretches its roots straight into the ground to store

5〜6mm
(0.23 inches)

nourishment. The seeds possess small wings to enable them to be easily blown away by wind, but because of the harsh environment, many of them will not grow. Only a very small portion of them can. The ones you see in Mt. Fuji are the lucky ones, adapting to the environment and managing to grow. This species develops "patches."

Meigetsu-sou (*Reynoutria japonica f. colorans*)
Polygonaceae, Reynoutria
Height: about 50cm (19.68 inches)

The meigetsu-sou and ontade are sometimes confused for one another.

Fuji-hatazao (*Arabis serrata*)
Brassicaceae, Arabis
Height: 10～30cm (4～12 inches)

  This is an indigenous plant of Mt. Fuji named after the mountain itself. To absorb more light for photosynthesis, it spreads its leaves like rose petals on the ground, giving it the generic designation of "rosette plant," which is also the most well balanced shape for the alpine zone. To avoid being blown away, even by a strong wind, it plasters itself over the ground. Moreover, it can move along with landslides. Even when a landslide occurs and severs some of the roots, thanks to a fine root system, it is still able to grow. Fuji-hatazao can retain its green leaves even in frosty temperatures, and photosynthesize earlier than any other plants in the alpine zone.

7. Flora of the Mt. Fuji Habitat

Around the Fifth Station (Subalpine Zone)

In this area, woody plants are common. The central part of the patch (P.53) becomes overcrowded with time, and as it expands the middle dies out sooner than the outside, leaving a patch shaped liked a donut. This furnishes a great environment for the seeds of woody plants and trees to grow, thanks to a setting that is both rich in nutrients and protected from the wind. This is truly a remarkable example of how a plant's hardiness can enable it to withstand even a cruel natural environment.

Kara-matsu, Japanese larch

(*Larix kaempferi*)
Pinaceae, Larix
Height: Generally, 20 ~ 30m (66~ 98 feet)

The conifers near the fifth station are Japanese larches, which have many interesting characteristics.

First, this tree can survive in dramatically hostile conditions.

Second, in normal conditions (around the fifth station), the larches grow straight up for over 20 meters (66 feet). However, around the vegetation limit, the shapes change completely and they begin to resemble "bonsai" trees. The main explanation for this is that in order to withstand the strong wind at this elevation, they have adapted by growing closer to the surface of the ground. With their unusual body shape, they have an amazing ability to survive. Please do not forget to compare the different shapes of larches when you visit the area around the fifth station.

Lastly, most of the conifers in Japan are evergreen, but in winter the larches shed their leaves. In autumn, the color of Mt. Fuji changes to gold and leaves us with a dramatic impression.

7.Flora of the Mt. Fuji Habitat

Miyama-hannoki, Japanese Alder

(*Alnus maximowiczii*)
Betulaceae, Alnus
Height:5 ～ 8m (16 ～ 26 feet)

If you walk slowly through the forest near the fifth station, you may smell a sweet scent like delicate cinnamon wafting through the air. Its source is actually the alder, which possesses the distinctive characteristic of having pleated leaves. The scent is thought to be its self-defense mechanism against insects and other enemies. Alders can grow in poor soil conditions because their roots contain nitrogen-fixing bacteria that can convert nitrogen into other forms used by living organisms. As "pioneer plants," they also contribute to ecological succession. Alders even nourish their own roots by dropping their nutrient-rich leaves onto the ground to decompose. By doing so, they are also contributing to the creation of the forest.

Vegetation in the Ochiudou
(Near the Fujiyoshida Entrance of the Fifth Station)

The Ochiudou is a walking-climbing trail along an area between the coniferous forest zone and the alpine zone on Mt. Fuji. This climbing route starts from the Fujiyoshida entrance. If you have even a little time, please consider taking a short stroll. You may even able to see some beautiful wildflowers.

Mame-zakura/ Fuji-zakura
(*Prunus incisa*)
Rosaceae, Prunus

Kokemomo
(*Vaccinium vitis-idaea*)
Ericaceae, Vaccinium

Murasaki-momenzuru
(*Astragalus adsurgens*) Leguminosae, Astragalus

7 Flora of the Mt. Fuji Habitat

Hakusan-shakunage, Alpine Rose

(*Rhododendron brachycarpum*)

Ericaceae, Rhododendron
Height: 1～2 m (3.3 ～ 6.6 feet)

Hakusan-shakunages are mostly seen at Ochiudou on the northern slope, from July to August during climbing season, with their big white and pink colored flowers.

Evergreen plants generally secrete a gloss into their leaves to extend their durability, just like when we wax and polish our car to take good care of it.

In the winter, rhododendrons curl and dangle their leaves. There are various plausible theories for why they do this, such as: by making them smaller, they can control the volume of moisture escaping from the leaves, and also lessen the extent of damage from the sunlight.

Interpretive GuideBook

Mountainous Area

Fuji-azami, Thistle

(*Cirsium purpuratum*)
Asteraceae, Cirsium
Height: 0.5～1m (19.68～40 inches)

In Japan, this largest species among the Cirsium genus produces a wonderful reddish purple flower with spiniferous leaves. They can sometimes produce up to 400 winged seeds that can be carried by the wind to more than 100 meters (328 feet) away for reproduction. Their distinguishing characteristic is that they can survive under harsh conditions and also extend their roots as deeply as 1 meter (3 feet) into the ground. This can stabilize the soil in the surrounding area, and help play a role in landslide prevention. In fact, grass establishment projects utilizing this concept are currently being undertaken to prevent landslides.

Plants are striving to stay alive. Let us observe them quietly without harming them.

Seeds of Thistle

7. Flora of the Mt. Fuji Habitat

Aokigahara Sea of Trees

Altitude: 920～1300m (3,020～4,260 feet above sea level)
Area: about 3,000 hectares

The "Aokigahara Sea of Trees" is a roughly 1,100-year-old forest formed on top of the lava that flowed when Mt. Nagao erupted in the year 864 (p.32). Generally speaking, it is a young and mixed forest, comprising both conifer and broadleaf trees.

Entering into this forest would likely produce a completely unique impression of a forest, compared to what most people would normally imagine. In this forest, most of the trees display their roots above ground, hugging each other like snakes.

Snake-like roots inside Aokigahara

There is a reason behind this. Because the earth below is covered with hardened lava, the roots are unable to penetrate into the ground. Amazingly, the soil of this forest is only several centimeters (1 inch) deep on average. For that reason, if a strong wind like that of a typhoon were to come, the trees would fall. But, this is just a cycle of nature. With the tree's demise, light can penetrate into the forest. And by decomposing into humus, the fallen tree will then hand over the torch of life to the next generation.

"In the forest, nothing is wasted. Everything has a purpose."

Photo: The Yamanashi Nichinichi Shimbun

7. Flora of the Mt. Fuji Habitat

Artificial Forest (The foot of Mt. Fuji)

About 70% of Japan's total surface area is forested. Of that, about 40% is "artificial" (or non-original) forest. Most of the forests you see in Japan are "artificial" forests of Japanese cedar and cypress. Why are there so many? After the Second World War, to help with the reconstruction effort, a huge area of forest was cut down and replanted with these conifers, which grow characteristically straight and tall.

Currently these forests remain largely untouched, with no light penetrating into them, and since most people use cheaper foreign timber instead of Japanese timber, they have essentially ceased to function as forests. Furthermore, these trees cause problems for many people with hay fever, which is an allergic reaction to pollen in the springtime in Japan.

Mixed forest of Japanese cypress and cedar

Sugi, Japanese Cedar

(*Cryptomeria japonica*)
Cupressaceae, Cryptomeria
Height: 30~40m (98~131 feet)

Sugi, or Japanese cedar, is very durable against water, easily processed, and also possesses such strength that, with some work, it can become a good building material. Many cedars can live for more than a thousand years in Yakushima Island.

Hinoki, Japanese Cypress

(*Chamaecyparis obtusa*)
Cupressaceae, Chamaecyparis
Height: 30 ~ 40m (98~131 feet)

The hinoki is famous as a material of the Houryuji temple that has been standing for 1300 years. Its wood contains an element of cadinol which is both aromatic and also prevents deterioration and protects against insects.

Currently in Japan, home construction utilizing Japanese timber is increasing in order to maintain Japanese forests.

8. Fauna of the Mt. Fuji Habitat

Mammals

Different kinds of mammals make their habitat in the hospitable environment around Mt. Fuji. There are currently 37 species identified to be living here, including rare species such as the Japanese serow and black bear.

Nihon-kamoshika, Japanese Serow

(*Capricornis crispus*)
Bovidae, Caprinae, Capricornis
(Special Natural Monument)
Body Length: 1～1.2 m (3.3～ 4 feet)

The Japanese serow is endemic, and almost like a dignified owner of the forest. They are herbivores and mainly eat leaves and grasses.

They move about in pursuit of food, inhabiting the cool alpine belt in summer and lower areas within the broadleaf forest in winter. If there are no leaves in winter, they eat the bark of trees.

The distinctive characteristic of the Japanese serow is its hooves. By spreading its two-toed cloven hooves, it can climb and also keep itself from falling down even very steep cliffs. Scientists think the "toes" of cloven-hoofed animals such as the serow, deer and boar have contracted over the course of evolution, in order to allow them to run faster.

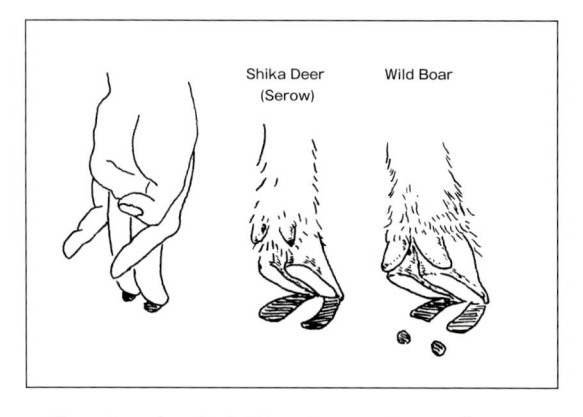

Shika Deer (Serow)   Wild Boar

To get a visual of this, please set your fingers as shown in the illustration, imitating their hooves. Put your index and point fingers on the flat surface. The rest of the fingers are used for support and balance. Like the "toe" of cloven-hoofed animals, your thumb (in a process of evolution) would diminish due to a lack of necessity and lack of use.

8.Fauna of the Mt. Fuji Habitat

Nihon-jika, Japanese Shika Deer(*Cervus nippon*)
Cervidae, Cervus
Body Length: 1〜2 m (3.3〜6.6 feet)

The Japanese shika deer is a well-known mammal for the Japanese, and is commonly seen at Mt. Fuji. They have been known to suddenly mosey out onto a road, and sometimes a bevy of females may stare inquisitively at us from the roadside. They are very active in the morning and early evening, and their diet is mainly grass. When the breeding season arrives in the fall, the males cry out "fee-fee," and the females reply. Entering the forest during this season allows you to listen to their amorous communication.

The male deer shed and re-grow their antlers every year. As they become older year after year, their antlers grow long, ramifying into branches, and upon reaching adulthood their antlers may contain up to four branches. These antlers are made of calcium. The antlers shed in the forest are also utilized by animals, such as rats, as a precious source of calcium. When wintertime comes around Mt. Fuji, and there are no consumable plants left for deer to eat, they turn to consuming the bark of trees instead of grass.

Unfortunately, the current ecosystem balance in most areas has shifted, causing the deer to move down through the forest and encroach upon cultivated fields.

Footprints

Faecal remains

Antler

8. Fauna of the Mt. Fuji Habitat

Inoshishi, Japanese Wild Boar

(*Sus scrofa leucomystax*)
Suidae, Sus
Body Length: 1～1.7 m (3.3～5.6 feet)

You may sometimes come across freshly dug ground beside a trail in the forest. This just may be the traces of a wild boar's digging with its nose to seek out plant roots and stalks, worms, and insects for food. You may also notice hoof prints or fallen hairs in a mud puddle. Boars sometimes roll around in puddles, daubing mud onto their bodies, which - when it dries, helps remove ticks and parasites. This kind of behavior is also performed by deer. The hoof prints are one way of distinguishing whether the puddle was used by a deer or a boar, since the boars leave prints of their sub-hooves in the mud (p.67).

You might notice rub marks on the rocks and trees around mud puddles.

No-usagi, Japanese Hare

(*Lepus brachyurus*)
Leporidae, Lepus
Body Length: 0.5~0.7m (1.6~2.3 feet)

Because the hare is a nocturnal animal, we rarely have the chance to meet them. Their diet consists mainly of bamboo grass. If you find the grasses sharply cut off low to the ground, it may be the field sign of a hare's having eaten there. More than anything, the distinguishing feature of the Japanese hare is its footprints. In the early winter's morning after a snowfall, you may find their tracks scattered all over.

Actually, the big footprint in front belongs to the back leg. With its small front legs it leans against the ground, bending its body like a prawn, and then it brings its back legs forward to the front. If you find its tracks, please try tracing them. You might be able to predict the hare's activities.

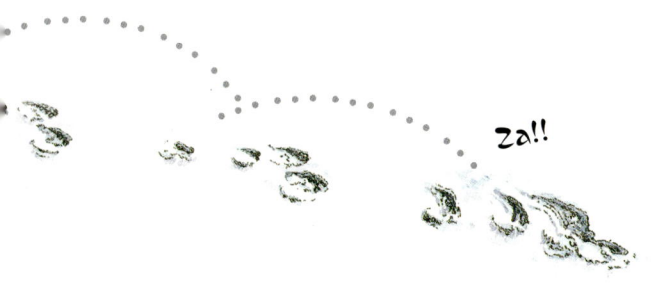

Za!!

8.Fauna of the Mt. Fuji Habitat

Nihon-risu, Japanese Squirrel (*Sciurus lis*)
Sciurinae, Sciurus
Body Length: 0.2 m (0.66 feet)

　If you were to stand quietly in the forest for a moment, you would probably hear a rustling noise coming from around the tree trunks. It might be a squirrel. They live in the trees of the broadleaf forest, feeding on acorns and conifer cones. Continue walking, and you might come across something interesting that looks just like a small Japanese "fried shrimp" on the rocks or fallen trees. This is actually the remains of an acorn that has been dexterously eaten by a squirrel.

　Squirrels have a habit of storing acorns by burying them, but since they often forget where they have buried them, it is often said that they are contributing to the restoration of the forest.

Which is the real thing?

Tsukinowa-guma, Japanese Black Bear

(*Selenarctos thiketanus japanicus*)

Ursinae, Selenarctos (endangered species)
Body Length: 1~1.7 m (3~ 5.6 feet)

The Japanese black bear has a trademark white crescent shape on its neck. It is an omnivore that mainly eats acorns, fruit, and honey, and sometimes insects and carrions. This bear is feared by humans since it sometimes preys on livestock and attacks people.

This bear is able to climb trees with its claws, and it eats the chestnuts and acorns found on piles of broken branches. The Japanese black bear is designated as an endangered species. They can still be found on the mainland of Japan, but they have disappeared on Kyushu and are on the edge of extinction on Shikoku.

8. Fauna of the Mt. Fuji Habitat

Living in Harmony with Wild Animals

Now we humans are facing huge problems between wild animals and us.

Wild bears frequently make appearances and cause direct injury and agricultural damage. Therefore, quite a number of bears are killed in Japan. Human activities are partially to blame. Decreasing the forests to cultivate food, and excessively developing the bears' natural habitat, invite easy access to depopulated villages, and call the bears into human living areas to feed on scraps.

On the other hand, the number of Japanese serows increased after they were protected as a Special Natural Monument. But, this action has actually caused them to encroach more into cultivated fields, due to increased populations, a shortage of food, and the loss of their natural habitat.

We definitely need to understand more about ecology and strive for coexistence between wild animals and humans.

Who ate these acorns?

The answer is P73.

Amphibians

Frogs (of which there are 43 different species living in Japan) eat insects and earthworms, and are preyed upon by other animals; therefore, if a place is inhabited by frogs, it's almost certainly possible to say that it is a biologically diverse area.

Mori-aogaeru, Forest Green Tree Frog

(*Rhacophorus arboreus*)
Rhacophoridae, Rhacophorus
Body Length: 5cm (2 inches)

The forest green treefrog lays its bubble-like eggs on tree branch, below which must be a puddle. Upon hatching, the tadpoles drop into the puddle where they will develop and mature. In places like Mt. Fuji where it is difficult for water to gather, even a small puddle presents a precious lifeline for frogs.

Azuma-hikigaeru, Japanese Toad

(*Bufo japonicus formosus*)
Bufonidae, Bufo
Body Length: 6 ~15 cm
(2.4~6 inches)

It can live in the alpine zone. During breeding season, many males flock around a female in small water area.

8.Fauna of the Mt. Fuji Habitat

Birds

The stretch of forest around Mt. Fuji, including the foothills, is inhabited by wild birds. Among the recognized 550 species found in Japan (including migratory birds), 130 kinds can be seen around Mt. Fuji.

Increasing altitude causes a drop in temperature, and for that wild birds too must seek to adapt their habitat to the environment. When you hear the wonderful twittering sound of birds, stop walking and remain quiet. These inquisitive birds just may come out to play.

Kakkou, Cuckoo (Cuculus canorus)
Cuculidae, Cuculus
Body Length: 35cm (13.8 inches)

These birds echo "cuckoo" across the bright forest bordered by grassland, which is usually quiet and far from human habitation. Therefore, when a store's business is not thriving, we say "the cuckoo is singing."

The cuckoo uses the nests of other bird species in which to lay its eggs, abdicating its role of incubating and fostering its chicks to other birds. Amazingly, the cuckoo chick kicks out the other bird's chicks from their nest.

Hoshi-garasu, Nutcracker

(Nucifraga caryocatactes)
Corvidae, Nucifraga
Body Length: 35 cm (13.8 inches)

Living high on the mountain, the nutcracker's white spots on its black colored body have earned him the Japanese naming of "hoshi garasu" or "star crow." These birds are mostly seen around the fifth station. They are omnivorous and have a habit of storing pine seeds by burying them to feed their chicks in winter.

Kakesu, Jay *(Garrulus glandarius)*

Corvidae, Garrulus
Body Length: 33cm (13 inches)

Its body is a pale grape color overall, with a part of its wing beautifully adorned with blue and black patterned stripes. It is quite skilled at imitating the sound of other birds. It is omnivorous and preys on the eggs and young of other birds. Though acorns are its favorite food, in autumn, by forgetting the place where it has buried them, it contributes toward the germination of the seeds.

8. Fauna of the Mt. Fuji Habitat

Ao-gera, Japanese Green Woodpecker

(*Picus awokera*)
Picidae, Picus
Body Length: 29cm (11.4 inches)

From inside the forest you can hear their sound: "tap tap tap tap." The Japanese green woodpecker, endemic to Japan, uses its pointed bill to pound noisily on wood surfaces to define its territory. Its whole body is covered in green, with a striped pattern along its belly.

Ama-tsubame, Swift

(*Apus pacificus*)
Apodidae, Apus
Body Length: 20cm (7.9 inches)

The swift flies "swiftly" overhead above cliffs, on crescent-shaped wings. It flies at high altitude in fine weather, going after insects for food, and at a low altitude when the humidity increases before the weather turns foul. When we see a swift flying at a low attitude, we predict that there will be rain. Swifts spend most of their lives, even sleeping and mating time, in the air.

Uguisu, Bush Warbler

(Cettia diphone)
Sylviidae, Cettia
Body Length: 15.5cm (6.1 inches)

The blue warbler is the most familiar bird for Japanese because of its call, a distinctive sound of spring: "Ho-Hoke-kyou." This sounds like the Buddhism Lotus Sutra, "Hokekyou," so some call it the "Hokekyou Bird". The droppings of the warbler, which contain lots of bleaching enzymes, have been used by the Japanese for stain removal on clothes, as well as for face-washes.

Ruri-bitaki, Red-flanked Bluetail

(Tarsiger cyanurus)
Turdidae, Tarsiger
Body Length: 14cm (5.5 inches)

This is a beautiful bird with a sapphire back and an orange stripe on its flank. They are not too afraid of humans, but it is difficult to find them, even with their distinctive color, since they prefer the dim groves. In the breeding season it normally inhabits the sub-alpine area, singing its melancholy trill.

8.Fauna of the Mt. Fuji Habitat

Kogara, Willow tit

(Parus montanus)
Paridae, Parus
Body Length:12.5cm (4.9 inches)

 This cute little bird looks as though it is wearing a beret and bow tie. It is very friendly and sings "hohi-hohi," as it approaches. It subsists on a mixed diet including insects and seeds, and lives in the lower part of the coniferous forest in summer and in the middle part in winter. Its small but strong beak can crack open tough nuts to eat the flesh.

Higara, Coal tit *(Parus ater)*

Paridae, Parus
Body Length: 11cm (4.3 inches)

 This smallest tit in Japan can be heard singing from the tips of coniferous trees. It is recognized by its black face and white cheeks. With its thin, clear voice, it repeatedly sings "choping-choping." In winter, coal tits often join mixed-species flocks that travel together in search of food. It is believed that an advantage of this behavior is increased awareness, and better detection, of predators.

Misosazai, Wren

(Troglodytes troglodytes)

Troglodytidae, Troglodytes
Body Length: 10.5cm
(4.1 inches)

This small bird weighs only 10 grams, about the weight of ten 1-yen coins, but it sings a prolonged melody that echoes through the forest. Utilizing moss, and sometimes the hair of deer and raccoons, they build their nests on the ceiling of caves.

Even in a harsh environment, wild birds help each other and live in harmony.

Therefore, even small environmental changes can cause a threat to their lives. Spring and summer are the breeding season for most birds, so try not to make much noise in the forest. If frightened, the birds might abandon their babies. Please do not forget that the forest is their home, and try to appreciate their hospitality in allowing you to trespass in their home.

Comparison of birds' size.
Scale: Sparrow

8.Fauna of the Mt. Fuji Habitat

Insects

In Japan there live more than 100,000 kinds of insects like beetles, grasshoppers, cicadas, dragonflies, bees, and more. On Mt. Fuji, insects are mostly seen at the altitude of 700~1,600 meters (2,997~5,250 feet).

Here, we will introduce several kinds of butterfly that get carried up by the wind blowing from the foot of the mountain to the midway.

Asagi-madara, Chestnut Tiger

(*Parantica sita*)
Danainae, Parantica
Forewing Length: 40~60mm (1.6~2.4 inches)

The chestnut tiger is a beautiful, relatively large butterfly with vivid patterning on its wings. Going north in the spring, and moving back south in the fall again, it is a migrating butterfly. It was discovered to have traveled about 1,800 kilometers (1,120 miles) over the ocean, from Taiwan to Japan. Moreover, It has a beautiful eye-catching body color throughout all of its life stages. It also equipped itself with the good sense to eat poisonous grasses during its larva stage and suck flower nectar during its adult stage to protect itself from predators.

Interpretive GuideBook

Ki-ageha, Old World Swallowtail

(Papilio machaon)
Papilionidae, Papilio
Forewing Length: 36~70mm
(1.4~2.8 inches)

Most species of this large-sized butterfly possess a projection at the back of the wing, and its larvae possess a horn that emits a bad odor to protect themselves from outside enemies. It is normally seen at the foot of the mountain.

Larva Stage

Monshiro-chou, Small White

(Pieris rapae crucivora)
Pierinae, Pieris
Forewing Length: 30mm
(1.2 inches)

It announces the coming of spring and is mostly seen in organic cabbage farms. Because of its small body, it can easily ride on the wind up to the alpine belt of Mt. Fuji.

Kujyaku-chou, Peacock

(Inachis io geisha)
Nymphalinae, Inachis
Forewing Length : 26~32mm (1.0~1.3 inches)

It is a beautiful butterfly named geisha that lives in the alpine belt.
There is a big eye-shaped pattern on its wings, believed to be used for threatening its enemies.

9.Present Condition of Mt. Fuji

Environment Conservation Activities

Every year 300,000 visitors come to Mt. Fuji during climbing season. And many volunteers join environmental conservation activities. Let's work together to preserve the beauty of Mt. Fuji

Climbers are always conducting volunteer rubbish collecting activities. Should you find any rubbish, please collect it, and pat yourself on the back for returning a favor to Mt. Fuji.

In most of the mountain huts, environmentally conscious toilets have been installed. These "bio-toilets" utilize bacteria to decompose human waste. After decomposition, the remains are brought into town and utilized as fertilizer.

To rehabilitate the forests caused by typhoon damage around Mt. Fuji, many volunteers are conducting replanting activities.

The Mt. Fuji Charter

The Governors of Shizuoka and Yamanashi Prefectures agree to the following aims to preserve the natural environment of Mt. Fuji.

- Learn about and be familiar with the nature of Mt. Fuji and be thankful for its abundant gifts.

- Cherish and protect its beautiful nature, thus cultivating an enriched culture.

- Strive to reduce the burdens on the natural environment and live in harmony with Mt. Fuji.

- Each individual should actively work towards preservation of its environment.

- Pass on the nature, scenery, history and culture of Mt. Fuji to future generations

18 November, 1998
Shizuoka & Yamanashi Prefecture

10. Mountain Climbing Information

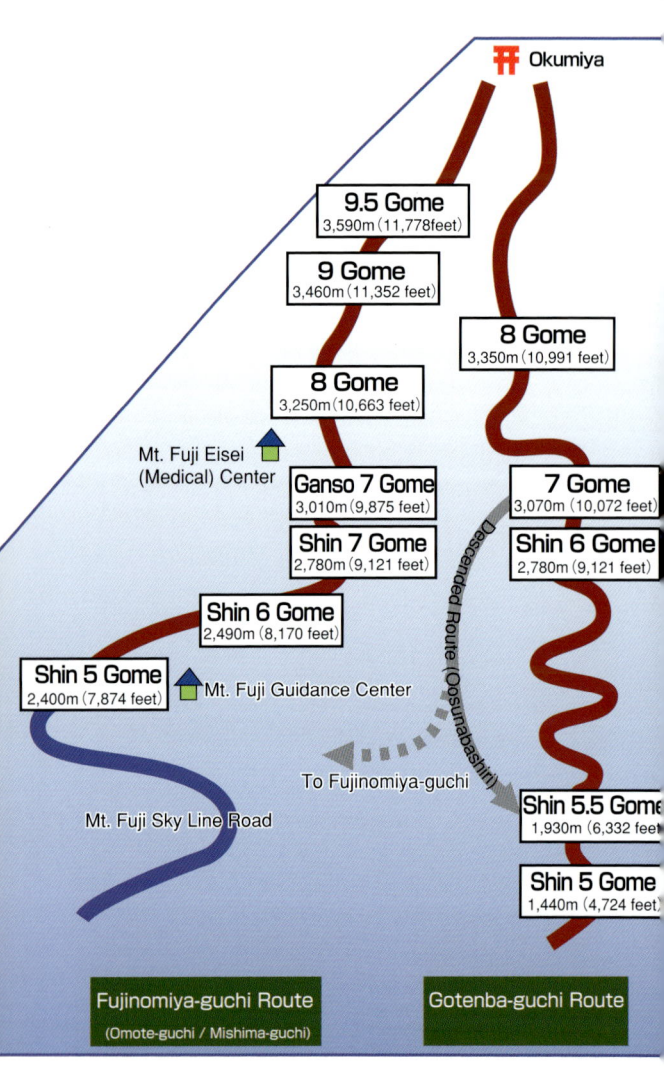

⛩ Okumiya

9.5 Gome 3,590m (11,778feet)

9 Gome 3,460m (11,352 feet)

8 Gome 3,350m (10,991 feet)

8 Gome 3,250m (10,663 feet)

Mt. Fuji Eisei (Medical) Center

Ganso 7 Gome 3,010m (9,875 feet)

7 Gome 3,070m (10,072 feet)

Shin 7 Gome 2,780m (9,121 feet)

Shin 6 Gome 2,780m (9,121 feet)

Descended Route (Oosunabashiri)

Shin 6 Gome 2,490m (8,170 feet)

Shin 5 Gome 2,400m (7,874 feet)

Mt. Fuji Guidance Center

To Fujinomiya-guchi

Mt. Fuji Sky Line Road

Shin 5.5 Gome 1,930m (6,332 feet)

Shin 5 Gome 1,440m (4,724 feet)

Fujinomiya-guchi Route (Omote-guchi / Mishima-guchi)

Gotenba-guchi Route

Emergency Contact Number

■ Shizuoka Prefecture

A call for help, mountain information and climbing report:
Fujinomiya-guchi, Gotenba-guchi and Subashiri-guchi

● Shizuoka Pref. Police: TEL. 054-271-0110
● Mt. Fuji Guidance Center (Open from Mid-July to Mid-August)

Interpretive GuideBook

Kusushi Shrine

9 Gome 3,600m (11,811 feet)

9 Gome 3,600m (11,810 feet)

Hon 8 Gome 3,400m (11,155 feet)

Hon 8 Gome 3,400m (11,155 feet)

8 Gome 3,350m (10,991 feet)

8 Gome 3,020m (9,908 feet)

Hon 7Gome 3,250m (10,660 feet)

Descended Route (Sunabashiri)

Descended Route

Mt. Fuji First-Aid Station

7 Gome 2,950m (9,678 feet)

7 Gome 2,700m (8,860 feet)

6 Gome 2,700m (8,858 feet)

Mt. Fuji Safety Guidance Center

6 Gome 2,390m (7,841 feet)

Sunabarai 5 Gome 2,300m (7,546 feet)

5 Gome 2,305m (7,562 feet)

Prefectural General Center

Komitake Shrine

Fuji Subaru Line Road

Shin 5 Gome 2,000m (6,562 feet)

Fujiyoshida-guchi

Kitaguchi Hongu Fuji Sengen Jinja

Subashiri-guchi Route

Kawaguchiko-guchi / Fujiyoshida-guchi Route

■ **Yamanashi Prefecture**

A call for help, mountain information and climbing report:
Kawaguchiko-guchi / Fujiyoshida-guchi

● Yamanashi Pref. Police: TEL. 0552-35-2121
● Mt. Fuji Safety Guidance Center: TEL. 0555-24-6223
● Prefectural General Center (5th Station): TEL. 0555-72-1477

10. Mountain Climbing Information

Climbing Season

July 1 to August 26. From August 10 until about August 20, because of the Japanese holiday season, there are car restrictions. Please contact information center ahead of time.

Condition of mountain climbing course

Because Mt. Fuji is a volcanic mountain, in some places you will be forced to walk through fine scoria (p.53). If they get into your shoes, it will be difficult or possibly painful to walk; because of this, we suggest wearing trekking shoes.

Average temperature at the summit

The average temperature at the summit in July is 4.5° C (40.1° F), and in August it reaches to just below 6° C (42.8° F). Strong wind may also dramatically cool your body temperature, so please make sure to prepare yourself against the cold.

How to climb

Walk slowly and maintain your own pace. Also, going down may be slippery, so try walking with short steps without lifting up your heels.

Falling Rocks

Falling rocks may often occur. If you cause or encounter falling rocks, please shout loudly "RAKUSSEKI!!!" to notify people below.

Altitude Sickness

The air pressure at the summit is only about 2/3 of that at the ground level. For this reason, at around 3,000 meters (9,850 feet) or above, some people may suffer from altitude sickness, of which symptoms may include headache and nausea. If this occurs, it is best to start descending the mountain. To avoid altitude sickness, try to breathe deeply and adjust your body to the altitude by walking slowly, and drink water as often as necessary.

Lightning Strike

Lightning is likely to develop during summer. Check the weather forecast and plan appropriately. If lightning occurs, descend immediately and/or take refuge in a hut for safety.

10. Mountain Climbing Information

Carry-on items:
Be prepared your safety climbing!!

	Checklist	Comment	☑
CLOTHING	Long-sleeved T-shirt	ideally quick-drying	
	Extra T-shirt		
	Underwear		
	Warm Clothing	ideally quick-drying fleece or wool to retain body heat	
	Sports Tights/Long Johns	jeans are not recommended due to possibility of rain	
	Trekking Shoes	ideally high-top and water resistant	
	Thick socks		
	Rain Gear	pants and jacket are preferable to a poncho	
	Hat	for sun protection	
	Knit Cap	for warmth and protection	
	Gloves		
EQUIPMENT	Backpack	a waterproof cover may be useful	
	Water Bottle (1L)	about 1 liter - refillable at the different stations along the way	
	Snacks	crackers, candies, chocolate, etc.	
	Map & Guidebook	don't forget to bring this book!	
	Headlamp	for night climbing - and don't forget to bring spare batteries!	
	Hand Towel or Bandana	for wiping hands/face	
	Plastic trash bags	please take your trash back with you	
	Watch		
	Tissues	biodegradable	
	First-Aid Kit	adhesive bandages, aspirin, prescription medications, etc.	
	Insurance Card	In case of emergency	
	Mobile-phone	In case of emergency	
OTHER USEFUL EQUIPMENT	Pen and paper		
	Walking Stick	very useful going both up and down	
	Spats	to keep ash and gravel out of your shoes	
	Sunglasses	for protection from dust and sunshine	
	Sunscreen		
	Lip Balm		
	Camera		
	Canned/Bottled Oxygen	to alleviate altitude sickness	

Interpretive GuideBook

Basic Information of Mt. Fuji

Yamanashi Prefecture

【Fuji Visitor Center】
Phone: 0522-72-0259
http://www.yamanashi-kankou.jp/fujivisi/fujivisi011.html

【Fujikawaguchiko Tourist Information】
Phone: 0555-72-6700
http://www.fujisan.ne.jp/index_e.php

【Fujiyoshida Tourism Information Service】
Phone: 0555-22-7000
http://www.city.fujiyoshida.yamanashi.jp/div/english/html/index.html

Shizuoka Prefecture

【Mt. Fuji Tourism Exchanges Bureau】
Phone: 0545-64-3776
http://www.fujisan-kkb.jp/english/index.html

【Shin-fuji Station Sightseeing Information】
Phone: 0545-64-2430

【Fujinomiya Sightseeing Association】
Phone: 0544-27-5240
http://www.city.fujinomiya.shizuoka.jp/english/

【Fujinomiya City Office】
http://www.fair-fujinomiya.com/mt.fuji/fujitop.htm

Walking sticks are sold at every station, and if you like you can pay a nominal fee to have a commemorative seal engraved in it at each one. Though they may be somewhat unwieldy, why not take your walking stick home with you for a great souvenir?

11.Closing Remarks

Whenever We guide a tour group around Mt. Fuji, particularly within the Aokigahara Sea of Trees, I always tell them that whenever a tree dies, its remains furnish the soil for the next generation of life coming after it. We humans may not be able to bequeath life to the generations after us in quite the same way, but we can have an impact on the future by sharing the message of respect for life with those around us.

Think about the place where you live, your surroundings. In recent times, our eyes have been opened to the numerous environmental problems springing up around the world, such as deforestation and over-fishing for commercial purposes. Although humans have respected the nature and culture around them for years, recently we have begun to embrace lifestyles and practices that are not sustainable. It is vital that we cast a glance back to our heritage and live mindfully, in harmony with the earth as much as possible, lest we strip it of all its richness.

As each of us, wherever we live, examines the local culture around us and humbly tries to learn from the generations that have come before, we just may discover a solution to today's distressing environmental problems. Even a small change in attitude or approach can yield great results, as we each endeavor to contribute whatever we can to make the world a better place.

Our desire is that every visitor who comes to Japan may be able to understand how deeply we Japanese revere Mt. Fuji, not only geologically or biologically, but culturally as well. As we embrace the task of conserving the area around this national treasure, which is also a point of national pride for us all, my appeal to you is this: please take heed to attend to the protection of the nature and culture of your own surroundings, in your own country and region. If every one of us does their part, I feel hopeful that the beauty of this Earth of ours can be preserved well into the future.

Authors

Interpretive GuideBook

About the Authors

Masanori Shintani (Environmental Interpreter) earned his Master of Environmental Science degree at the Florida Institute of Technology.

He has more than 15 years of experience as an interpreter and trainer in the field of ecotourism, and has worked in the Mt. Fuji area as well as overseas, including Hawaii. He currently lives with his wife and three daughters at the foot of Mt. Fuji in a traditional Japanese home which he built himself, along with the help of a carpenter friend. A recipient of the prestigious Mt. Fuji Scout Award (the highest attainable rank among the Boy Scouts of Japan),

Mr. Shintani is also the representative of Eco-Logic as a consultant of ecotourism and environmental education activities around the world and a Mt. Fuji ecotour guide.

www.mtfuji.asia

Toshio Tagami (Artistic Interpreter) has worked as an interpreter within the Visitors Center at Fuji Hakone Izu National Park. His works focusing on aquatic environments have been added to collections in the United States, Spain, Korea, and elsewhere. Using his skill as an artist, he awakens people's curiosity to discover the precious living creatures in the natural environments immediately surrounding them.

www.toshiotagami.com

Public Collection ▶
by Tagami

Water Rings 62X81cm Colored Pencil

11 Closing Remarks

ACKNOWLEDGMENT

Many people have assisted in turning our desire to write this interpretive book about Mt. Fuji into reality. We would like first to thanks Dr. Shigeo Aramaki, Head of Yamanashi Institute of Environmental Sciences, for making a correction of volcanic chapter, Mr. Yoshitaka Koda at Fujisan Hongu Sengen Taisha, for cultural chapter, Ms. Hiroko Hirotani for Flora chapter and Mr. Teruo Katsuyama for Fauna chapter, Museum attendants of Kanagawa Prefecture Museum of Natural History, and Mr. Hideo Kageyama, Member of Wild Bird Society of Japan, Minami Fuji Branch, for birds chapter.

We would also like to thanks organizations who has allowed their pictures to be published and supported to look for them, Yamanashi Institute of Environmental Sciences, Fujinomiya City, Town of Fujikawaguchiko, Fujiyoshida Kankou-shinkou Service, Fuji-nishiki Saké Brewery, the Yamanashi Nichinichi Shimbun and Lake Tanuki Nature School.

Our special thanks to Mr. Shigeharu Otaki, Shizuoka Shimbun, who had spent much effort in the book's production, Ms. Kayoko Nagakura, Shizuoka Shimbun, who were responsible for time consuming task of produce the book. Ms. Audrey Heald, Mr. Andy Smith, and a representative for ENGLISHBOX, Mr. Noriaki Fukushima, who had supported my English writing and given a lot of passion to us and Ms. Lisa Brochu and Mr. Tim Merriman, who taught me the real meaning of "interpretation".

Finally, I would like to deeply thank our wives and children to support over the year.

Authors